I0017788

Chapter 1: Introduction to Laptop Repair & Maintenance

Getting to Know Your Laptop

Before attempting any of your own repair or maintenance, it is essential to get familiar with the specific make and model of laptop you are working with. Different laptops have different components, sizes, and wiring. Gathering the necessary knowledge is the first step in laptop repair or maintenance. You should read through the user manual of your laptop so you can better understand the inner workings and components of your laptop. Be sure to look into the safety instructions in your user manual before attempting anything yourself. It is also important to gather the right tools before undertaking any laptop repair or maintenance. Having the right tools and parts comes in handy and can make your job much more efficient. It is important to have the right screwdrivers, antistatic gloves, cleaning materials, and other such items. You should also have a toolset specifically designed for laptops, which will come in handy if you need to disassemble the laptop.

Safety Considerations

Due to the fragile nature of laptops and their sensitive components, it is important to be extra careful and aware when attempting any laptop repair or maintenance. A laptop is made of highly intricate parts and wires that can easily be damaged, so it is crucial to take every necessary precaution in order to protect it. To keep your laptop safe, you should make sure to discharge any static electricity before touching it. Wear antistatic gloves, as recommended in the user manual, to minimize risk of electrostatic discharge (ESD). Ensure your work area is free of liquids or other materials that can damage your laptop. If you are disassembling the laptop, make sure to store each component correctly and securely.

Basic Repair Tools

When it comes to repairing or maintaining your laptop, having the right tools and parts comes in handy. A laptop is made up of intricate components and wires, so you need to be sure that the tools you use are of the highest quality and appropriate for the job. You should also have a toolset for laptops, which is typically made up of a medium Philips and flathead screwdrivers, ESD safe tweezers, and other such tools. It is also beneficial to have an expanding collection of parts, such as a power supply connector, cooling fan, expansion port cover, laptop battery, and more.

Laptop Anatomy

Having an understanding of the anatomy of a laptop is necessary for any laptop repair or maintenance. All laptops have similar components, but the arrangement and size may vary depending on the make and model. Becoming familiar with the laptop's anatomy can help you identify potential problems and necessary repairs or upgrades. The main components of a laptop are the display, motherboard, RAM, processor, hard drive, audio chip, network card, and other peripheral devices. The design of a laptop is complex, so the various components are typically connected with cables and screws. Opening the laptop and carefully removing pieces, such as the display panel, can give you a better understanding of how each component is situated and connected to the other. This can help to identify any components that may need to be replaced or upgraded. In conclusion, it is important to become familiar with the make and model of your laptop. This includes reading the user manual and safety recommendations, gathering the necessary tools, and getting to know the anatomy of the laptop. With the right knowledge, tools and parts, you can successfully repair and maintain your laptop.

Chapter 2: Basic Troubleshooting

Understanding Your Operating System

With the enormous amount of operating systems available today, it can be hard for laptop owners to understand how to best maintain their system. While some are more familiar than others, such as Windows and Mac OS, it's important to understand the basics of your operating system and how to access important software and security settings. No matter the OS, the most important element is to ensure the laptop is up to date and has all the appropriate drivers installed. It is recommended that laptop owners check the support page of their laptop's manufacturer regularly to ensure they are on the latest operating system and have downloaded the latest set of drivers available.

System Settings & Updates

In addition to staying up to date with the latest version of an operating system, laptop owners must also pay attention to their system settings. This includes ensuring the laptop is configured to the owner's desired preferences. Also, it is crucial that certain security settings are enabled in order to protect the laptop from potential malicious threats and keep the data on the laptop secure. System updates are often released to patch security loopholes, so laptop owners should ensure their system is regularly updated with the latest version for optimal security.

Common Issues & Fixes

Simple laptop maintenance can often go a long way in solving potential system and hardware issues. Basic maintenance requires laptop owners to keep their hard drive clear of unnecessary files and data, keep the laptop cleaned and dust-free, and remove any unnecessary software. While regular cleaning and maintenance of internal and external components should be performed to ensure optimal performance. Some external components such as power adapters, mice, external screens and the like should also be tested or replaced periodically. should be tested and replaced periodically.

Diagnosing Hardware Issues

If a laptop appears to be operating slower than usual or hardware is malfunctioning, the laptop owner should attempt to identify any faulty, damaged, or disconnected components. Troubleshooting hardware issues are one of the most complex tasks of laptop repair and maintenance. It is advised that laptop owners diagnose issues with caution and properly label and disconnect any components they may not be familiar with. This can help avoid further damage to the device and make further diagnosis and troubleshooting easier. In some cases, it may be necessary to request assistance from a qualified technician to perform a deeper assessment and locate the precise source of the problem.

When a laptop appears to be operating at an abnormal speed or is affected by unexpected system behaviors, it is important to attempt to diagnose the problem as quickly as possible. It is also important to identify any laptop issues before installing new software or updating the system in order to ensure installation won't make the problem worse. If a laptop's hardware appears to be malfunctioning, it is advised that laptop owners disconnect any external devices and check the device's support page to locate any potential fixes. In some cases, it may be best to only have essential hardware connected to the laptop in order to locate the source of the issue. In the event laptop owners are unable to locate any issues after performing the necessary diagnostics, they should seek assistance from a qualified technician. He or she can use specialized tools and techniques to determine the problem. Once the issue is located and fixed, laptop owners should remember to regularly back up their data and keep their devices free of dust and debris. This can help prevent future system issues and extend the life of the device.

Chapter 3: Battery maintenance

Maximizing Battery Power

It goes without saying that the most important factor to consider when it comes to laptop battery maintenance is maximizing the battery power. After all, the whole point of laptop maintenance is to make sure your device has enough juice to get you through the day. Here are a few tips for achieving and maintaining maximum battery power:

-Optimize the laptop's settings for maximum battery life. This includes reducing the brightness of the display, disabling network connections and sleep mode, and shutting down hardware and programs that aren't in use.

-Don't let the laptop get too hot. A laptop should never exceed a temperature of 90°F, and unplugging the laptop from its charger can help keep the internal temperature lower.

-Try to avoid draining the battery completely. Discharging a battery all the way can reduce its capacity and lifespan, so try to charge your laptop when the battery is running low.

- Properly store the battery. If the laptop isn't going to be in use for an extended period of time, the battery should be removed and stored in a cool, dry place.

Replacing Batteries

At some point, it may be necessary to replace a laptop's battery. This is usually necessary when a laptop's battery won't hold a charge anymore, or if the battery has become physically damaged. Replacing a laptop's battery usually requires removing the laptop's bottom plate, and can be a complicated process. As such, it's best to consult an experienced professional or take the laptop to a repair shop before attempting to replace the battery yourself.

Optimizing Charge Cycles

Charge cycles are one of the most important factors in maintaining the life of a laptop battery over time. Generally speaking, the more charge cycles a laptop battery goes through, the shorter its lifespan will be. Optimizing charge cycles means making sure the battery isn't being overcharged or over-discharged. This can be done by making sure the laptop isn't left connected to its charger all the time, and refraining from draining the battery all the way.

Enhancing Charging Efficiency

Enhancing charging efficiency is another important factor to consider when maintaining a laptop battery. It's important to make sure the charger being used is the right type for the laptop; using a charger that has the correct connection and voltage will help make sure the battery is being charged properly. Faulty chargers or incorrect chargers can cause damage to the battery, so it's important to use the right one. Additionally, it's important to clean the laptop's charging port from time to time, as dirt and debris can accumulate and prevent a solid connection. Following these tips and guidelines can help ensure that a laptop's battery stays healthy for as long as possible. Taking the time to care for a laptop battery properly ensures it will keep working for years to come. Knowing the basics of battery maintenance is a key step in maintaining a laptop, and can help avoid costly repairs and replacements down the line.

Chapter 4: Hardware Maintenance

Cleaning & Upgrading the Keyboard & Mouse

Cleaning and upgrading a laptop's input devices is an important part of laptop maintenance and repair. Keeping the laptop's keyboard and mouse clean can help improve the performance of the laptop and extend the life of the equipment. There are a few key steps that can help extend the life and usability of a laptop's keyboard and mouse. Start with a soft, lint-free cloth and, if needed, a gentle cleaning solution or detergent can be used to wipe away any dirt, dust, and grime. Be sure to clean gently between the keys and under the mouse to ensure that no dirt particles become stuck in the keys or between the mouse buttons. Upgrade the keyboard and mouse with replacement parts if any of the components start to show signs of wear or damage. Experts recommend replacing the parts every two years and changing the keycaps or mouse buttons if they become sticky. Careful attention should be paid to the type of replacement parts that are purchased to ensure they fit with the laptop hardware.

Upgrading Memory & Storage

When it comes to laptop maintenance and repair, upgrading memory and storage is often a recommended solution for improving laptop performance. Increasing the RAM and storage ensures that the laptop is able to handle larger and more complex tasks without freezing or slowing down. Memory and storage upgrades are relatively straightforward, but users should always refer to the laptop's user manual for information on RAM and storage compatible with the laptop. Upgrading a laptop's RAM involves replacing the SODIMM memory sticks that are placed inside the laptop. The user should check the manual to find out how many RAM sticks the laptop can support, as well as the speed and type of RAM that is compatible. Upgrading a laptop's storage also requires checking the user guide. Laptop hard drives come in several different sizes, so it is important to purchase the right size and type of drive before beginning the installation process.

Common Component Issues & Replacements

When it comes to laptop maintenance and repair, some of the most common issues that arise are component related. Aside from the keyboard and mouse, a laptop's other components may require repair or replacement over time. Many of these components can be easily identified and replaced by the user with the help of a laptop repair and maintenance guide. A laptop's hard drive and power block are two of the most common component issues that need repair. Computer repair experts recommend checking and replacing the hard drive if there are any signs of data corruption or unsuccessful recovery. Replacing a laptop's power block is also a recommended solution for improving laptop performance and ensuring the safety of both the laptop and user.

Assessing Heat & Power Issues

Laptop heat and power issues can be caused by a number of factors. Heat is generated during use and is managed by cooling vents, fans and heat sinks. If any of these components become clogged or blocked, it can lead to a laptop overheating. Clogged vents can also cause a laptop to run slower as it is unable to dissipate heat efficiently. Many cases of laptop heat can be solved by cleaning the fans and vents or repositioning the laptop to ensure an ample amount of ventilation. Power issues can also affect a laptop's performance, so it is important to check the laptop's power sources and cables. Replacing the power adapter if it becomes frayed or damaged is a recommended solution for improving laptop performance and preventing power related errors. Checking the laptop's battery and ensuring that it is properly charged is also important. Contact a laptop repair company if there are any further issues with the laptop's power sources.

Chapter 5. Software Maintenance

Installing & Configuring Operating Systems

Installing and configuring an operating system on a laptop is a critical skill for any laptop repair technician. Many laptops come pre-installed with the operating system, but some may need an install process if it is going to be used for another purpose. It's important for a laptop repair technician to have an understanding of the installation process of each operating system, as well as the configuration and settings that are necessary to properly optimize the laptop for its intended use. Common operating systems include Microsoft Windows, Apple macOS, and Linux. The first step for a laptop repair technician is to obtain the necessary installation media, such as a DVD or USB drive, for the operating system. Once the media is obtained, it will need to be inserted into the laptop and the installation process can begin. During the installation, it is important to create the necessary partitions on the laptop's hard drive and to select the appropriate drive that will be used as the primary drive. Once the partitioning and drive selection process is complete, the laptop repair technician will need to install the necessary drivers and configure the operating system settings.

Customizing Software

After the installation of an operating system has been completed, it may need to be customized to meet the specific requirements of the user. This customization process generally involves the installation of additional software applications, such as productivity and security applications, as well as the configuration of the operating system to meet the user's preferences. For instance, the laptop repair technician may need to configure the system to enable wireless networking, install antivirus software, and install any other necessary applications. It is important to take the time to configure any applications properly so that the user can maximize the performance of their system. Additionally, the laptop repair technician may need to ensure that any security settings are appropriate for the user's particular environment.

Virus & Malware Detection & Protection

One of the most important roles of a laptop repair technician is to ensure the laptop is protected from viruses and other malicious software, or malware. There are several steps that can be taken to protect the laptop from these malicious programs, such as installing and running antivirus software, installing a malware detector, and regularly scanning the system with a reputable security application. When a virus or other malicious software is discovered on a laptop system, it needs to be properly removed. This process can be complex and often requires the use of a specialized anti-malware removal tool. It is important to use the appropriate malware removal tools and to not try to manually remove a virus, as this can often lead to more issues. Once a virus or malware has been successfully removed, the laptop should be scanned with a security application to ensure that all potential threats have been eliminated.

Troubleshooting Driver & Compatibility Issues

Another important skill for a laptop repair technician is to understand how to diagnose and troubleshoot driver and compatibility issues. This is a critical skill since many laptop systems have a variety of hardware components, from the display to the audio card, that may be incompatible with the current version of the operating system. Additionally, the technician will often need to troubleshoot issues with specific drivers and applications. In order to diagnose driver and compatibility issues, the laptop repair technician must first identify the underlying issue. Depending on the complexity of the issue, this may involve the use of specialized testing tools or diagnostic procedures. Once the issue has been identified, the laptop repair technician must then locate the appropriate drivers or applications and install or update them to ensure the laptop is functioning properly. Additionally, the technician may need to make any necessary adjustments to the laptop's system settings or hardware components as part of the troubleshooting process.

Chapter 6: Connectivity

Having a reliable and secure connection to the internet is essential for the modern laptop user. In this chapter, we'll discuss the basics of setting up Wi-Fi and charging, as well as exploring ways to set up and use your laptop's bluetooth and networking features. We'll also cover troubleshooting common connectivity issues, and discuss the benefits of cloud services and data storage solutions.

Wi-Fi & Charging

One of the most important things to keep in mind when using a laptop is to stay connected. Most laptops come with an inbuilt Wi-Fi card, which allows you to connect to local networks. You can also use an external Wi-Fi card, which is more versatile and offers more options. In order to keep your laptop charged, use a laptop adapter that's compatible with your model. Many laptops come with a dedicated charging port, which is typically located at the left or right side of the laptop. This port is used to charge the laptop battery with an external adapter. You should always use the proper charger for your laptop, as incorrect chargers can damage the battery or cause other problems.

Setting Up Bluetooth & Networking

Another great way to stay connected is by using your laptop's Bluetooth and networking capabilities. Bluetooth is a wireless protocol that allows devices to communicate with each other over a short range without the need for wires or cables. Once two devices have established a connection, they can exchange data back and forth. Most laptops come with a built-in Bluetooth card, but an external card can be added for increased range and coverage. Networking is available on many laptops and allows you to join a local area network (LAN) or connect to the internet. To set up a network with your laptop, you'll need an Ethernet cable and an internet modem or router.

Troubleshooting Common Connectivity Issues

Connection issues are among the most common laptop problems. If you experience difficulty connecting to the internet or other devices, try these tips first: • Check the connection settings of your Wi-Fi card or modem. Make sure the connection is enabled and that you're using the correct security settings. • Try troubleshooting the connection in the laptop's Network & Sharing Center. • Check the laptop's network adapter settings, to ensure there aren't any outdated drivers or compatibility issues. • Try restarting your laptop, or resetting the router or modem. • Contact your internet service provider (ISP) for assistance if needed. If you are using a public Wi-Fi network, make sure to take extra precautions with your security settings, and only visit sites you trust. If you're having difficulty connecting to a Bluetooth device, double-check the pairing and security settings, as well as the possibility that you are out of range.

Cloud Services & Your Laptop

Cloud services are becoming increasingly popular as a way to store, access, and share data from anywhere. A cloud service is a data storage and processing system that runs on a remote server. You can access the data from your laptop, as well as from other devices or computers. This type of storage is ideal for those who need to access large amounts of data from multiple locations. Using cloud services can help you save money, and can make data more secure and accessible. Many cloud services offer generous storage and a variety of features and flexibility. Furthermore, it's easy to back up files and documents, and these backups can be accessed from anywhere. Cloud services can also be used to access software and applications, stream music and videos, and sync data with other devices. For secure and reliable data management, cloud storage is an excellent option for laptop users. It's important to do some research and compare different providers before committing to a service, to make sure you are getting the features and options you need.

Chapter 7: Repairs & Upgrades

Part Selection & Replacement Tips

Many laptop parts can be replaced and upgraded without having to perform an entire rebuild or complex repair. Understanding how individual parts interact and function correctly is important when considering which components to replace or upgrade. To ensure your replacement/upgrade is successful, the following tips should be taken into account:

- Confirm the technical information for each part before you make a purchase. Parts may differ from one model to another and some may not be compatible within the same brand.
- If a part is labeled as a compatible replacement, double-check that the part will physically fit in the laptop, and if applicable, verify the potential operating temperature range.
- Check that the upgrade/replacement part has the same electrical rating as the original part. This will help in ensuring the correct current, voltage, and power requirements do not exceed those of the device.
- Be aware of the fact that some devices may include additional protection circuitry such as thermal sensors and other added lighting components which may have to be replaced in unison.

- For devices containing integrated parts such as CPUs and GPUs, verify the compatibility with the rest of the components on hand.
- Do not forget to remove dust and accumulated dirt from the laptop before installation. By doing this, the chances of electrostatic discharge (ESD) during installation can be reduced or eliminated.
- Power down the device and unplug it from all power sources before commencing any internal work.

DIY Maintenance & Repairs

The majority of maintenance and repair tasks can be completed by the user in the comfort of their own home. However, it's important to note that some tasks require specialized tools and knowledge which might be inconvenient or even dangerous for the inexperienced user. Safety should always be the foremost concern when performing any maintenance or repair activities. The most common DIY hardware maintenance tasks include:

- Dust and debris removal from fans, heatsinks and other components.
- Labeling and organizing of internal components for troubleshooting and/or replacement purposes.
- Cleaning of internal and external components using special cleaning solutions and solvents.
- Replacement of failed, damaged or malfunctioning components such as BIOS chips, capacitors, capacitors, connectors and more.

- Replacement of faulty cables and contacts such as SATA, USB and other connectors.
- Installation of upgraded components such as additional RAM, GPUs and SSDs.
- Testing and troubleshooting of components and circuitry with the use of specialized tools and test equipment.
- Installation of additional cooling fans, heatsinks and other cooling related components.
- Replacement and calibration of batteries.

While most tasks can be completed satisfactorily with minimal knowledge, one should consider seeking professional assistance for matters pertaining to bios flashing or tinkering with the system firmware. Additionally, certain types of repairs, such as thermal module replacements or soldering work, are best left to professionals.

Professional Repairs & Services

In many cases, complicated or difficult repairs may be too much for an unwitting user. In these cases, professional help should be sought. Professional laptop repair services can come in various forms. Alternatively, reputed repair centers may offer comprehensive repair packages or pick-up services for more involved repairs. Many professional laptop technicians can also be consulted online and via remote access services. Parts and components that are replacements for no longer available parts are sometimes available via refurbishment programs and specific webstores, allowing users to acquire rare parts quickly and at reduced costs.

External Repairs & Enhancements

Various external laptop parts, components and accessories have become available over the years, making it possible to enhance the existing performance of a laptop by upgrading or replacing certain parts. Depending on the model and series, some popular external laptop enhancements include:

- Bluetooth receivers/adapters
- External hard disk or solid-state drives
- External graphics or video cards
- USB multi-ports or docks
- Slim optical drives
- External storage enclosures
- Battery packs
- Heat sinks and cooling systems

In addition to the above, laptop users can enjoy many other unique accessories and peripherals available for various purposes such as a 2.4 GHz wireless mouse for gaming, or a USB keyboard and/or mouse for general use. Many of these accessories are uniquely engineered for modern-day laptops and can drastically improve the overall power and performance of the laptop. Certain laptop models, such as the MacBook Pro, even have their own specialized accessories, such as the MagSafe power adapter and the external GPU accessory, which add an additional layer of protection and convenience fine-tuned to the specific needs of the laptop user.

Chapter 8: Troubleshooting System Errors

Identifying System Errors

The first step to solving any system error is to identify what the cause is. If a laptop is not running correctly, the user must be able to recognize which component or hardware is causing the problem. By using tools like system logs, hardware diagnostics and hardware monitoring, it's possible to analyze the system's processes and identify the source of the issue. In some cases, the error may identify itself by displaying a message on the screen or in the system log. Other errors, such as system freezes and failed hardware, will require further investigation into the underlying causes and potential solutions.

Solving Common System Issues

When solving a system issue, it's important to understand the limitations of laptop hardware and software. Many laptop issues are caused by software incompatibilities or hardware instability. In cases like these, the user must troubleshoot the system to determine which component is causing the problem. In cases where the system is misconfigured, the user should check the configuration settings and ensure that all options are correctly set. It may be necessary to uninstall and reinstall components, or even reconfigure the system entirely.

Improving System Performance

Performance issues can be caused by both hardware and software issues. The user should check the system logs to identify any components that require maintenance or repairs. Performance issues can also be caused by low system memory, outdated drivers or software, or even by malware or virus infections. To improve system performance it's necessary to address each of these potential causes. Updating drivers and software, adding additional RAM, running anti-virus scans and removing unnecessary programs are all common methods for improving the speed and responsiveness of a laptop.

Chapter 9: Display & Graphics

For laptop owners who use their laptops for digital media, gaming or other intensive graphical tasks, having a strong display and stable graphics are essential. Display and graphics are among the most commonly-faulty components for a laptop, and repair and maintenance for these components can be difficult. Here, we will discuss assessment and repair tips, optimizing display settings and resolutions, upgrading video and audio components, and troubleshooting distorted graphics.

Assessment & Repair Tips

When assessing the display and graphics of a laptop, oftentimes the laptop's user manual or service guide can help pinpoint potential sources of failure. Many modern laptops will have diagnostic software installed, which is designed to check over the system and detect any issues in the display or graphics. These programs should be run promptly when experiencing any display or graphics issues. When attempting to diagnose the cause of a display or graphics failure, there are several components that should be checked first. Of particular note are the LCD panel, the backlight, the inverter board and the graphics card. The data and power cables connected to these components can also come loose, resulting in a blank or distorted display or sluggish system performance.

Optimizing Display Settings & Resolution

Having a properly sized display for the laptop's screen is essential for a comfortable viewing experience. Most laptops will have scaling options that allow the user to change the size of the display on-screen, typically expressed as dots-per-inch (DPI) settings that determine how large or small the windows and text appear. For example, a lower-resolution setting might look crispier on a large monitor, while a higher-resolution setting looks sharper on a smaller monitor. Within Windows, users can also adjust their display settings to optimize their laptop's display for brightness, contrast, and color. It is recommended to use the video card's control panel for making these changes, as this often provides the most accurate results.

Upgrading Video & Audio Components

For laptops that are designed for media playback, music production, or gaming, upgrading the video and audio components of the laptop can be necessary for smoother visuals and outstanding sound. Most laptops can support upgrades in the form of dedicated video and audio cards, which are typically installed to provide a high-performance experience. When upgrading these components, users should use caution to ensure they install the correct type of card. Additionally, if a laptop user is not experienced with installing these components, professional help should be sought to ensure the best performance.

Troubleshooting Distorted Graphics

Distorted graphics on a laptop display can be caused by several factors-from a damaged graphics card to a failing LCD panel. Troubleshooting these issues can be tricky, and often requires careful examination of each component involved in the display. In some cases, a laptop's graphics distortion might be the result of a damaged driver or incompatible third-party software. Updating the graphics driver or disabling the third-party software might resolve the issue. If a graphics card or driver is not the source of the issue, examining the display panel, inverter board, and data/power cables can also be necessary. If all else fails, contacting support or taking the laptop in for repair or replacement may be the only option. In conclusion, laptop display and graphics are some of the most important components for a laptop, and involve a delicate balance of onboard hardware, software, and even third-party components. When encountering display or graphics issues, it is essential to properly diagnose the source of the problem before attempting repairs or upgrades, as this can save the user time and money.

Chapter 10: Data Security & Recovery

Data security and recovery are important components of laptop maintenance and repair, enabling users to keep their systems, data, and private information protected from hackers and malicious viruses. Data security and recovery apply to the maintenance of the security of computer and network systems, as well as protecting data from accidental or intentional loss or damage.

Installing & Updating Security Software

Computer and network security is essential to protect against malicious attacks, such as viruses and infiltration. To help protect laptops and other computers, it is important to use a secure system such as Windows Defender, McAfee VirusScan, Norton Antivirus, or Kaspersky Internet Security. This can help to protect laptops from potential risks as well as protect personal data. Appropriate security software should be installed and updated regularly, if available.

Diagnosing Data Loss & Recovery

If data is lost due to hardware or software failure, it may be possible to recover it using recovery software or by hiring a professional data recovery service. If the data is not recoverable, users should document what was lost and how it can be replaced in order to minimize any losses.

Best Practices for Data Security

Data security and recovery should be a priority for all laptop users. While it may be appealing to use free or trial versions of antivirus software, users should consider investing in a reliable and robust security suite that is constantly updated to protect against the most current threats. Additional measures such as password protection and data encryption can also help to secure personal files and information. If a laptop is shared between multiple users, there should also be a clear division of the responsibilities of protecting data.

Chapter 11: Troubleshooting Audio & Video

Diagnostic & Repair Tips for Audio & Video

Troubleshooting audio and video issues is all about finding the origin of the problem as quickly as possible, in order to fix it before it becomes a major issue. When dealing with audio and video problems, a professional technician must be able to identify and narrow down the potential sources of the issue in order to make a repair or adjustment with confident assurance. Start by identifying what type of device is giving you problems. Whether it is an integrated system, a connected external device, or a plug-in

Once you clarify the source, the next step is to locate the affected components—including digital display panels and cables—as part of troubleshooting protocol. A qualified laptop repair technician should be familiar with the onboard audio/video components and have the appropriate tools to identify and fix the problem. When troubleshooting audio and video problems, the technician should first determine whether the issue is hardware- or software-related. When dealing with a hardware-related issue, it is important to assess whether or not the hardware is compatible with the laptop. If so, then the problem may be with the connections or cables.

When dealing with software-related issues, the technician should check for corrupted drivers and any Windows updates that may be required. Furthermore, the technician should check to see if any new software has been installed that may have caused an incompatibility with the laptop's audio and video components.

Troubleshooting Compressed Files

When dealing with compressed audio or video files, such as those found in media players, the technician should understand what these files are, how they are compressed and why they may give you an error. For instance, audio and video files that contain a lot of data are compressed using a variety of technologies, including MPEG-1, MPEG-2, and MPEG-4, to reduce their file size and thus become more manageable for transmission. Compressed video files can also be used in editing software, whereby multiple shots can be combined into one file. If any of these compressed files are corrupted or corrupted by a virus, it may lead to playback issues or errors. Fortunately, the prospective technician can remedy these problems by running antivirus and antispyware checks and by downloading the appropriate codecs for playing the video format.

Troubleshooting Audio Devices

Any laptop repair technician who specializes in audio and video should have expertise in troubleshooting various audio devices, such as speakers, headphones, microphones, and DACs (digital-to-analog converters).

Generally, audio devices require more troubleshooting than video equipment, due to the complexity of the sound waves. When troubleshooting audio devices, the technician should first check the compatibility of the device to the laptop, as some devices may be compatible but may not work due to incompatibilities with software or drivers. Additionally, the technician should take into consideration any external components, such as cabling and/or issues with the power supply, which may be required in order to get the audio device working.

Configuring Audio Output

Another important area of laptop repair and maintenance when dealing with audio and video is configuring the audio output. This means setting the desired output for audio devices, such as speakers and headphones, as well as testing any external audio hardware, such as receivers and mixers. This requires the technician to have a good grasp of the differences between digital and analog signals and the differences between each type of audio system, such as 2.1, 5.1, and 7.1 surround sound. Furthermore, the technician should have knowledge of audio settings such as LPF (low pass filter) and HPF (high pass filter) and how to apply these settings in order to get the most from the audio devices.

Chapter 12: BIOS & Firmware

Basic Input/Output System (BIOS) is responsible for booting up the computer. It is software stored on a chip in the motherboard that manages data flow between the system's hardware components and the operating system, as well as providing a user interface for users to configure hardware settings preferences. Firmware is a software program embedded on a hardware device which provides the necessary instructions for configuring, programming, and controlling the device. When it comes to laptop computers, maintaining and updating the BIOS and firmware are essential for the smooth and safe operation of the computer.

Understanding the Basic Input & Output System

The BIOS performs a number of important tasks during the system startup process. It first verifies the system has the necessary and compatible components to support boot up, such as CPU, memory, video, and hard drive. It then loads the basic operating system Settings and starts the computer in the operating system's normal operating state. The BIOS also stores important information regarding the configuration of system components, such as memory and hard drive settings, as well as provides instructions for the system on how to access those components.

The main interface of the BIOS is usually a text-based menu, where users can configure system settings, as well as set passwords and set security options. Typically, system administrators can configure the BIOS using

the keyboard and mouse or using a software utility, such as the Advanced
Configuration and Power Interface (ACPI).

Updating & Maintaining Firmware

Firmware is often preloaded on laptops, which means that user updates
are not needed in order to keep the laptop running optimally. However,
updating the firmware can often times improve security and functionality,
making it a beneficial practice. Updates are typically available from the
manufacturer's website and can be installed by downloading the update
and running the installation program.

Firmware updates for certain components, such as the video card or
network interface, can have a large impact on the overall performance of
the system. Performing regular firmware updates can help keep the laptop
up-to-date with the latest security and performance enhancements.
Additionally, since some firmware updates can be quite large, users
should ensure that they have a reliable internet connection before
attempting to update their firmware.

Troubleshooting BIOS Errors

When BIOS errors occur, they will usually prevent the laptop from properly connecting to the operating system or peripherals. The most common BIOS errors are memory and hard drive errors, which can be caused by defective hardware or incorrectly configured system settings. In such cases, the user should first check for any compatibility issues between the laptop and the device causing the error. If the problem persists, it is often best to reset the BIOS settings to their factory settings and attempt the installation again.

If the BIOS is not functioning properly, the user may need to update the BIOS with a new version from the manufacturer's website. This should be done with extreme caution, as some BIOS updates may damage the system if performed incorrectly. Additionally, certain BIOS settings should only be changed by experienced users and system administrators, such as updating the security options or enabling hardware features.

BIOS Security

Most laptops have security options available in the BIOS to help protect the system from unauthorized access. It is important to set a strong password on the BIOS, as any unauthorized user who is able to gain access to the system's BIOS settings can make permanent changes that could be detrimental to the system or users. Additionally, many laptops also utilize drive encryption and secure boot settings, which can be configured through the BIOS. Enabling these settings can help protect the system from malware and other malicious software.

To protect the BIOS from being modified by unauthorized users, most manufacturers allow users to password-protect the BIOS. Additionally, some laptops have an administrator password that allows the user to limit access to certain parts of the BIOS. This can be used to restrict access to advanced settings, such as changing the security settings or enabling hardware features, to users who are knowledgeable about the system. When it comes to laptop repair and maintenance, maintaining the BIOS and firmware are essential for the optimal and secure operation of the laptop. Keeping the BIOS updated to the latest version can ensure that the system is running properly and that security and performance settings are up-to-date and running smoothly. Additionally, setting strong passwords on the BIOS, as well as drive and boot settings, can help protect the system from unauthorized users.

Chapter 13: Software Installation & Configuration

Having a laptop that runs on the latest software is important for optimal performance. However, installing and configuring the right software for your device can be time-consuming, difficult and risky. Therefore, it is important to understand software installation basics, configure applications, as well as setting up remote connections for optimal performance.

Choosing & Downloading Software

When it comes to choosing and downloading software for your laptop, it helps to do some research to ascertain the compatibility. You can do this by checking the specifications of the device against those of the software's requirements. Before downloading any software, ensure to read the system requirements to make sure your laptop meets the minimum requirement for installation and use. It is also important to pay close attention to the exact version of the software you download as many of the applications have different versions that may be incompatible with your laptop. If you are unsure of the exact version of the software to download, a great starting point would be to carefully read the release notes that are output by the developers. Once you have established the right version of the software to download, you can proceed to download it from official websites.

Installation Basics

After selecting the right software for your laptop and downloading it, the next step is to install it on your device. Depending on the software, the setup process can be quite easy or complicated, and may require you to input detailed information. It is important to pay close attention to the setup process to ensure no components are omitted by mistake. Pay attention to the required settings and permissions to avoid leakages and privacy breaches. Pay attention to the computer's app store as well. This is important because download stores can provide additional information about particular software. Ensure you read the reviews that are available to get insights on the application before you run the installation. Also, going through the EULA can help you determine the limits of use, which is critical to determine the functionality of the software.

Configuring Applications

In most cases, software requires a certain amount of configuration before they can be used productively. There are several settings and options that may need to be customized according to the type of software you are dealing with and your preferences. Configuring applications allows users to customize how their laptop operates, as well as how certain software works.

A few of the common settings include the following:

• Security Settings: Configuring applications involves changing the security settings to ensure that the laptop is secure and there are no malicious activities. This includes setting up authentication measures and managing access to the device.

• Data Sharing: This involves setting up methods of data exchange with other users and systems. You can specify the type of data you want to share with others, which accounts should have access, and what types of documents can be uploaded to the system.

• Notifications: With the right settings, you can receive notifications about updates and other important information. Setting these up correctly will help ensure your laptop is updated with the latest software and patches.
• Customization: Customization options allow users to personalize how the applications look and feel. This could include creating personalized wallpaper backgrounds, setting system colors, and customizing the menu bar.

Setting Up Remote Connections

In addition to installing and configuring applications to effectively manage your laptop, you may also need to set up a remote connection. Remote connections enable users to access their laptop, regardless of the location. This can give users access to important files and systems whenever they need them, while providing the added advantage of increased security. The first step to setting up a secure remote connection is to select the appropriate security protocol and setup. Depending on the types of files you wish to access, you may choose to use a virtual private network (VPN).

This allows users to access their network without compromising security, as VPNs provide encryption for data being transferred. Once you have chosen a security protocol, configure the applications to use the connection. This process involves tweaking a few settings and providing your usernames and passwords. It is important to use strong passwords to secure your data and systems. Test the connection after configuring the settings to ensure it is working properly. Finally, ensure the access to your laptop is limited to those who have permission.

Set up an authentication and access control system to restrict access to your network and systems, keeping it safe from malicious intentions. With these steps, you can set up remote connections for your laptop easily and securely. With the setup in place, you can access your laptop from any location without compromising the security of your data and systems. Leverage the power of remote access to stay productive and securely maintain control over your laptop.

Chapter 14: Networking & Security

One of the most important aspects of laptop repair and maintenance is ensuring the network settings and security are fully optimized. This chapter will provide an introduction to networking and security-related topics, and also discuss the various steps to ensure the proper functionality of a laptop and secure user data.

Establishing Network Settings

Establishing the correct network settings can be critical to the successful operation of a laptop. The settings must be able to connect to any available wireless networks within range and detect any available hardwired connections. They must also route traffic through the most efficient paths for any web content needed by the user. Additionally, settings such as DHCP and IP addresses must be properly set. For novice users, the most straightforward way to set up networking settings is to use the built-in utility software provided by the operating system. This can usually be found on the Control Panel and includes a simple wizard for configuring network settings. More advanced users may wish to manually configure their network settings. In these cases, it is critical to ensure that the correct settings are chosen in order to ensure the efficient routing of network traffic and prevent data breaches.

Creating & Managing Passwords

To ensure secure access to a laptop, it is important to establish and maintain strong passwords. The most secure passwords are random combinations of letters, numbers, and special characters, and they should be changed regularly. Additionally, it is a good practice to avoid using the same password for multiple accounts. For users with multiple accounts, using a password manager can come in handy. These programs store a user's passwords securely and allow for easy management. They also make it easier to generate strong passwords, which are much more difficult to guess than simple words.

Enhancing Security Settings

Security settings should also be regularly checked and updated to ensure the highest level of protection. This includes enabling data encryption, setting up software and system updates, and enabling firewalls. Additionally, users should make sure that any software that is installed on their laptops is from a reliable source and does not contain any malicious code. It is also important to be aware of any potential risks posed by users connecting to unsecured public networks. Whenever connecting to a public network, it is recommended to ensure that a Virtual Private Network (VPN) is used to ensure a secure connection.

Adjusting Firewall & Proxy Settings

Firewalls and proxy settings are important to ensure a secure connection to the internet. Firewalls can be used to block unwanted incoming and outgoing traffic to the laptop while also preventing malicious code from entering the system. For users with a dedicated internet connection, proxy settings can also be used to increase the security of their connection. These settings allow the laptop to connect to the internet through a third-party server rather than directly to the internet. This helps to shield the user from potential malicious activity by making their IP address masked. By properly establishing, managing, and adjusting their network settings, users can ensure the optimal performance and security of their laptops. Knowing the proper steps for networking and security allows for more reliable and secure networking sessions, improved performance and updated software and hardware. Finally, with the proper network and security settings, users can typically enjoy a worry-free and enhanced laptop experience.

Chapter 15: Backups

Protecting Against Data Loss

Protecting your data is essential for the success of any laptop repair and maintenance project. Simply backing up your data through cloud storage services or to an external hard drive can save you a ton of time and money should something happen to your laptop. Additionally, there are many software solutions and hardware devices available to help protect your data in the event of a hardware or software malfunction. Utilizing firewalls and anti-virus tools to monitor your system can also help prevent hackers and malicious software from obtaining your sensitive information. Finally, whenever making changes to your laptop or data storage system, it's always good practice to create multiple backups and test their integrity before making any changes to your system.

Chapter 16: Troubleshooting Software

Software malfunctions can be one of the most frustrating and difficult types of problems a laptop user may face. Whether it be general system errors, driver problems, or issues with the user interface, tracking down and resolving software problems can take time and patience. In this chapter, we'll discuss the basics of troubleshooting software errors and provide tips on managing software resources to help your laptop run at optimum performance.

Diagnosing Software Problems

The first step in resolving software-related issues on a laptop is to diagnose the possible causes. Troubleshooting software errors is often a complex process, so it's important to first consider the specific symptoms you're experiencing. Are there system errors or crashes? Is the laptop failing to load certain software? If so, what type of application is it? Understanding the nature of your problem can help you identify the root cause and allow you to better troubleshoot and fix the issue. In addition to considering the type of software you're running and the specific symptoms you're experiencing, it's also important to make sure that the laptop itself is running properly. Ensure that all hardware devices are functioning correctly and that any external devices are connected properly. Check that your laptop is free from dust, dirt, and other debris that can cause hardware malfunctions and impede system performance.

Troubleshooting Drivers

Computer drivers are the software that enables hardware devices to communicate with the operating system. Drivers may need to be updated when new hardware is installed or when existing hardware needs to be repaired or replaced. They typically come as part of the hardware device package, but they may also be available through the laptop's manufacturer website. To troubleshoot issues related to drivers, it's important to make sure that all of the necessary drivers are installed and up-to-date. The best way to do this is to identify the hardware components installed on your laptop and then verify that the corresponding drivers are correctly installed. If drivers are not present or are expired, you'll need to download and install the correct drivers from the hardware vendor's website.

Managing Software Resources

In addition to ensuring the correct drivers are installed and operational, it's also important to maintain a clean and organized list of software resources. Unneeded software can take up valuable space and slow down your laptop's performance. To maintain optimum performance, it's important to regularly review the list of installed applications and remove or disable any that are unnecessary. Don't forget to also review the laptop's startup applications. Many laptops come preloaded with a variety of applications that start when the laptop is powered on. Reducing the number of these startup applications can greatly improve system performance and bypass unnecessary functions.

Resolving User Interface Issues

User interface issues can also cause frustration and disrupt your work or entertainment. If you're having trouble navigating on your laptop, it may be due to a corrupted driver, outdated software, or a corrupted system profile. To resolve user interface issues, it's important to update your laptop's drivers, disable any unnecessary software, and then restart the computer. If these steps don't work, you may need to create a new user profile or discuss the issue with a qualified technician who can qualify the issue. Software errors and malfunctions can be a real nuisance when using a laptop. But with the knowledge and tips outlined in this chapter, you should be able to effectively troubleshoot software errors, update drivers, and manage software resources. By following the tips outlined in this chapter, you'll have a greater chance at keeping your laptop running smoothly and avoiding costly repairs or downtime.

Chapter 17: Servers & Storage

Network Configuration & Storage Semantics

Configuring a network for a laptop is one of the more complex tasks in laptop maintenance and repair. Setting up a laptop on a network requires configuring the wireless connection, a system administrator's permission, knowledge of the local area network (LAN), and proper authentication. It also requires configuring the server, which is crucial for any laptop to communicate with its environment. An understanding of server settings and storage semantics is vital to guaranteeing secure, reliable, and efficient data transmission. Once the server is up and running, it is equally important to know how to configure it to allow for the necessary type of file sharing. This is accomplished by creating a folder structure that follows certain standards. The structure is based on standards like the Common Internet File System (CIFS) protocol, as well as the Access Control List (ACL) protocol. It is important to keep in mind that these standards must be followed in order to successfully configure the server.

Hard Drive Maintenance & Replacements

Having a reliable hard drive is critical for laptop maintenance and repair. Hard drives can fail for a variety of reasons, and it is important to be familiar with the tools and techniques used to diagnose and repair them. Common problems can include mechanical failures, software or firmware issues, or physical damage. In addition, it is also important to be able to identify signs of imminent failure, such as unusual noises, slow performance, or strange error messages. Fortunately, a large number of tools are available for hard drive maintenance and repair. These include disk imaging software, disk eraser utilities, disk scrubbers, and secure wipe programs. Each of these tools has its own particular suite of features, so it is important to select the one that best fits the laptop's needs. In addition, it is always important to make sure that any upgrades or replacement drives are compatible with the laptop's hardware.

Storage Encryption & Security

For any business or individual using a laptop, it is essential to maintain a secure storage system. Laptop security must include both physical and digital security measures. When it comes to digital security, secure encryption is essential for any sensitive data or information stored on the laptop. Encryption is the process of transforming data so that only people with the right keys can access it. This can be accomplished through a variety of methods, such as public/private key encryption, symmetric/asymmetric key encryption, or one-time passphrases. For laptops, the most common encryption method is Advanced Encryption Standard (AES). It is important to note that different software and hardware systems may support different encryption methods, so it is important to research the best one for each system.

Server Troubleshooting

Laptops can often become overwhelmed by server issues, ranging from slow loading times to complete system freezes. In order to diagnose and repair server issues, a technician must be familiar with a variety of networking tools, such as ping and traceroute utilities, and have a good understanding of the underlying networking protocol. In addition, it is important to be able to identify the source of the problem. There may be an underlying software configuration issue, a hardware component that needs to be replaced, an incorrect network configuration, or an external factor such as an unusually large network traffic load. In order to properly diagnose the problem, a technician must be able to collect and analyze data from the server, as well as compare it to baseline data to determine if it is within acceptable parameters. Once the source of the problem has been identified, the technician can then begin to formulate a plan of action to resolve the issue. This may involve updating software, replacing hardware components, ensuring proper security settings, or changing settings on the server to optimize the performance. No matter what the situation is, it is important to document all changes for future reference.

Chapter 18: Maintenance Strategies

Maintaining a laptop requires much more than just a regular software and hardware check. It requires careful planning, quick decisions, and the right set of tools. There are many strategies that professionals use to keep their laptops running smoothly and efficient. In this chapter, we'll discuss some of the best practices for laptop upkeep and look into the tools used for troubleshooting. We will also look into the importance of examining wear and tear.

Best Practices for Laptop Upkeep

One of the best ways to keep your laptop running in top condition is to follow a regular maintenance plan. It's important to regularly check the hardware and software to make sure everything is up to date. Additionally, it is important to update any drivers or software, check for virus and malware, and clean out any dust buildup in the machines. This can go a long way in preventing a breakdown and ensuring your laptop will last for a long time. The first step is to ensure that all your software and hardware are up to date. This means making sure that any software programs, such as Microsoft Office, are up to date. It's also important to update any antivirus and malware programs as well. This will help to keep your laptop secure and free from any potential threats. In addition to keeping your software and hardware up to date, it is also recommended that you backup all of your important data on a regular basis. This helps to ensure that your data is safe and secure in the event of any unforeseen breakdown.

This is especially important for those who do a lot of work on their laptop and need to have their files available at all times.

Timetable for Regular Maintenance

In addition to regular maintenance, it's also important to create a timetable for maintenance. Depending on how much work you do, you might need to change the timeframe for your maintenance schedule. However, it's always a good idea to check your laptop on a regular basis. Depending on the severity of any problems, you might decide to perform a complete reset each month or a simple reset every other month. It is also a good idea to pay close attention to any changes in the performance of your laptop. Any technical issues should be addressed as soon as possible by a professional laptop repair technician. It is also important to read up on any new software updates and make sure that you're running the latest version.

Troubleshooting Tools

In order to identify any technical issues, it's important to have the right tools for the job. The most common tools used for troubleshooting purposes are diagnostic software and system utility tools. Diagnostic software can be used to scan for any issues, such as a broken hard drive or an infection from a virus. Meanwhile, system utility tools can be used to fix any errors, such as fragmented files or corrupt system settings.

Examining Wear & Tear

Wear and tear are inevitable when using a laptop on a regular basis. It's important to regularly check for any wear and tear, such as scratches or dents, to ensure that they are not compromising the performance of your laptop. Any serious damage should be addressed by a laptop repair technician as soon as possible. In addition to checking for any wear and tear, it's also important to check on any water or liquid damage. If any liquid gets into your computer, it can cause irreparable damage if not addressed immediately. It's important to be aware of any potential liquid spills and address them immediately. Finally, it's also a good idea to check your laptop for any heat damage. Laptops can get quite hot, especially during heavy use. It's important to check the fans and vents to ensure that they are working properly and not overheating the laptop. If anything appears to be off, it's best to turn the laptop off immediately and either contact a technician or attempt to troubleshoot it yourself. Taking the time to maintain your laptop on a regular basis will go a long way in ensuring its longevity. It's important to keep it in the best condition possible, which requires both regular maintenance and a keen eye for any potential issues. It's important to take a preventive approach rather than a reactive approach when it comes to laptop upkeep. By planning ahead, you can help to prevent any serious issues from occurring.

Chapter 19: Cleaning & Care

Cleaning and caring for your laptop doesn't need to be a difficult task. By taking the time to properly maintain your laptop and clean it regularly, you can prevent dirt, dust, and other build-up from affecting your laptop's hardware and software.

Cleaning & Dusting Tips

Start by making sure your laptop is turned off and unplugged before cleaning. If you haven't already, consider getting a can of compressed air and gently dusting off the vents of the laptop and the hard-to-reach places in between the keys and crevices of your laptop. Never spray compressed air directly onto the laptop. Instead, gently dust in the direction of the vents. When finished, use a soft cloth to lightly wipe away any dust that may have been dislodged from the laptop. Don't forget to clean your laptop's screen. To protect the LCD surface of the screen, use a damp cloth and a mild non-abrasive cleaner such as eyeglass cleaner. Gently wipe away any dust or dirt and then use a dry cloth to wipe away any residue. Taking your laptop to a professional cleaner is also an option.

Tips for Protecting & Maintaining Your Battery

Replacing your laptop battery should be done every 3 to 4 years depending on the type of batter and how often it is used. To ensure your battery lasts as long as possible, use the following tips: • Keep your laptop cool by making sure it's not exposed to too much heat or direct sunlight. • Try to avoid leaving your laptop plugged into an outlet constantly; only plug it in when the battery is low. • Don't forget to power down your laptop when not in use; having the laptop in a state of constant sleep drains the battery quickly. • If possible, keep your battery charged between 40-80% as this can help to extend the battery's lifespan.

Tools for Cleaning & Care

There are many tools you can use to properly maintain and clean your laptop. A can of compressed air can be used to remove dust from hard-to-reach spots. Microfiber cloths are ideal for dusting and cleaning the laptop's surface. Q-tips dipped in isopropyl alcohol can also be used to clean hard-to-reach areas around keyboards and other crevices. Finally, a cotton swab dipped in hydrogen peroxide is great for removing any residue left on your laptop's surface. Taking the time to properly care for and maintain your laptop is essential in order to ensure a long life and the best performance. With a few simple maintenance tips, you can ensure that your laptop is running efficiently and performing well.

Chapter 20: Cooling & Ventilation

Evaluating Cooling Components

The cooling system of any laptop poses one of the most important considerations when determining overall system health and performance. As laptop internals generate more and more heat from the use of more powerful processors, graphics cards, and memory, the thermals need to be taken into account to ensure that the temperatures remain within acceptable levels. Evaluating the cooling elements of a laptop is carried out simply by removing the components of the laptop and analyzing their condition. Dust and debris build up around fans, heat sinks, and venting systems, so that needs to be thoroughly cleaned on a regular basis. When inspecting the fan, any loose solder joints or damage to the connectors should be noted, as the course of action will then dictate the type of replacement part that will be needed. The fans need to be tested to determine their operational speed and also to ensure that they are spinning as they should. The laptop's CPU and GPU temperatures also need to be checked as well, as they can be adjusted with proper airflow and cooling. It is imperative to understand what the appropriate temperature is for the components and throttle points, as it can be detrimental to the whole laptop if these are exceeded.

Upgrading Fans & Coolers

A common problem with laptops is a decrease in performance that can be attributed to inadequate cooling. The thermal paste that helps the processor to dissipate heat may break down over time and no longer conform to the processor and heatsink properly, leading to an increase in temperatures and a decrease in performance. Replacing the thermal paste with a new one and also replacing the existing fan with a cooler, quieter one are two good upgrades that can be made to reduce the running temperature of the laptop. The replacement of fans or coolers is a relatively straightforward process, as they are usually secured with screws or bolts and can be replaced in the same way. Some recommended coolers are those that come with PWM (pulse width modulation) control, which will allow the fan to run at a lower speed and reduce noise, while also having the capacity to increase speed under certain load conditions.

Improving Airflow & Ventilation

Apart from upgrading fans, an effective method of improving cooling is to consider the airflow of the laptop. Poor airflow through the laptop's vents can lead to an increase in temperatures, which can then lead to components being damaged or degraded in performance. Installing external fans is one good way to improve ventilation, as is using laptop stands and riser pads to elevate the laptop slightly and allow for better airflow. Additionally, the fan vents on the outside of the laptop can be kept clean as dust and debris can clog them and hinder airflow. It is also worth noting that a clogged heat sink within the laptop can also prevent the cooling system from being able to work efficiently.

Diagnosing Heat-related Issues

When a laptop starts to overheat or its performance is beginning to degrade, it is important to diagnose the issue and determine the cause. After evaluating the cooling system and making any necessary improvements, the next step is to run diagnostic utilities to identify where the issue is located. Heat-related problems can be difficult to diagnose, as they can often be the result of multiple components or combination of low airflow and low cooling capacity. CPU applications such as Prime95 or FurMark can be used to stress the system and identify any thermal issues that may be present. On top of that, checking CPU and GPU temperatures and monitoring clock speeds can also be useful in identifying problems, as well as using the laptop's performance test to see if any components are beginning to struggle due to the heat. As far as overheating is concerned, it is worth performing any repairs or upgrades in intervals so that it can be tracked to identify whether a particular improvement has helped to reduce the temperature of the laptop. Poor cooling can be one of the leading causes of laptop failure, so understanding how the cooling systems of a laptop works and also having an appreciation for the heat generated by today's components is paramount for keeping a laptop running for years to come.

Chapter 21: User Error & Safety

When it comes to laptop repair and maintenance, it is essential for IT technicians and users alike to be aware of the risks posed by user errors and safety problems. In this chapter, we will examine how best to assess user errors and safety risks as well as how to teach users how to troubleshoot and detect problems on their own. We will also discuss ways of making user safety a priority and optimizing user safety.

Assessing User Error & Safety Risks

Evaluating user errors involves recognizing the potential risks posed by user actions, such as downloading malicious software, hardware not being plugged in properly, or not following manufacturer instructions. These errors can lead to a variety of problems such as data loss, system slowdowns, or permanent hardware damage. To minimize the risk of user errors, IT technicians should conduct periodic assessments of user-generated data and user workflows as well as regularly monitoring user behavior to detect any suspicious activities or errors. User-generated data should be regularly backed up by IT technicians to mitigate the risk of data loss in the event of accidental deletion. It is also recommended for users to take the precautions to avoid data loss by creating multiple backups and storing those backups in secure locations. It is also important for IT technicians to stay up-to-date on the latest security software and patch releases and to test and deploy them as necessary.

Teaching Diagnosis & Troubleshooting

It is not enough to simply protect users from the risks posed by user errors; IT technicians must also teach users how to diagnose and troubleshoot their own laptops. By providing users with the necessary knowledge and skills to identify and solve problems, IT technicians can reduce the risk of user errors by ensuring that any problems that may arise can be resolved quickly and with minimal disruption. Teaching users how to diagnose and troubleshoot their laptops involves providing users with a comprehensive guide that explains the different areas of laptop repair and maintenance and how to perform each task. This guide should provide step-by-step instructions on how to troubleshoot hardware and software and should also include any relevant contact information for hardware vendors or other companies that might be able to assist the user. Additionally, IT technicians should provide regular tutorials or seminars on diagnostics and troubleshooting to ensure that users are up-to-date on the latest strategies and technologies.

Making User Safety a Priority

User safety is not only important for protecting users from user errors, but also for mitigating the risks posed by hackers and cyber criminals. Educating users on cyber security best practices is an important part of ensuring user safety and avoiding any potential data breaches or malicious activities. IT technicians should provide users with comprehensive cyber security training and advice on how to protect their laptop from potential threats. Additionally, IT technicians should regularly monitor user activity and employ appropriate measures such as regular password updates, firewall configuration, and malware scans.

Optimizing User Safety

Finally, IT technicians should always strive to optimize user safety by keeping users up-to-date with any new security information and technology advancements. IT technicians should implement regular maintenance and upgrade cycles to ensure that laptops are running the latest versions of software and that any outdated hardware is replaced with more secure alternatives. Additionally, IT technicians should also make sure that laptops are protected by a reliable antivirus program and that firewalls and other security measures are regularly updated and configured correctly. Finally, IT technicians should ensure that users are kept informed of any new security threats or vulnerabilities, and they should always be available to help users if they need assistance or have any questions.

Chapter 22: Working Remotely

As technology continues to advance and more workplaces become increasingly globalized, the opportunities to work remotely and take advantage of remote access technologies increase. For laptop repair and maintenance technicians, understanding how to set up and use remote workstations, establish secure connections and troubleshoot remote access are essential skills.

Setting Up Remote Workstations

Establishing a secure remote workstation is the key to successful remote access. Before connecting to a remote environment, all necessary security measures should be taken into consideration. This includes installing up-to-date anti-virus software and a firewall, as well as setting up and updating a list of allowed users. Encryption protocols and authentication techniques should also be in place. Once connected, it's important to check the strength of the connection regularly. In addition to ensuring a secure connection, network administrators should also be sure to install robust remote access software that is capable of performing various maintenance and repair tasks. This could be anything from a remote desktop sharing program to a system monitoring tool. Tools like these make it much easier for technicians to diagnose and repair any issues that may arise.

Encrypting Remote Connections

Another important step when setting up a remote workstation is encrypting all remote connections. This ensures that data exchange between the remote workstation and the laptop is kept secure and confidential. This encryption can be done with various encryption technologies such as SSL or IPsec. Before selecting a specific encryption protocol, it's important to discuss the benefits of all potential options with an IT expert. Encrypted connections are great for protecting all data transmitted and received over a remote connection, however, to further boost security, remote workstation administrators should also consider configuring VPNs on clients' laptops and using two-factor authentication. Doing so will increase the overall security of the remote connection and ensure that only authorized users have access.

Troubleshooting Remote Access

In order to provide technicians with the best remote access experience, troubleshooting issues should always be the first priority. Issues with remote connections can be due to technicalities such as connectivity issues, poor latency or low bandwidth or could be due to authentication problems such as incorrect username and password. It's important to test the connection before attempting to repair any issues and use dedicated tools such as ping or traceroute to measure the performance of the connection. Technicians should also be sure to investigate any error messages or warnings that may appear during the connecting or authentication process. It's important to understand the cause of the issue and then find the appropriate solution. Once the issue is fixed, technicians should always be sure to test the connection again to ensure the issue is resolved.

Taking Advantage of Online Services

There are many online services available to assist with laptop repair and maintenance. Remote access capabilities allow technicians to take advantage of these services to diagnose and repair issues remotely. This saves them both time and money, and also minimizes the risk of any physical damage to the laptop. Some of the most popular online services include remote storage solutions and software diagnostics tools, both of which can be accessed from anywhere with an internet connection. Online services can also be useful for online collaboration. Services such as Microsoft Teams or Slack allow technicians to work together remotely, finding solutions and troubleshooting issues. This can be especially effective when technicians have to evaluate large datasets or participate in extended troubleshooting sessions. Understanding how to use remote access is a key skill for laptop repair and maintenance technicians. By taking the time to properly set up and secure remote connections, as well as troubleshoot any potential issues and make use of the many online services available, technicians can ensure a smooth, secure and efficient remote experience.

Chapter 23: Communications & Networking

Wireless Networking Basics

Wireless networking has become increasingly common in the computing world. With the vast array of available wireless routers and adapters, setting up a wireless network is becoming increasingly easy and accessible to users of all tech backgrounds. Wireless networking is the communication process of two or more devices that are within a certain range of one another to communicate through wireless signals. This type of communication is usually enabled by a wireless router, which acts as a bridge between your laptop/devices and the internet. Before we get into setting up a wireless network, understanding the network basics can help improve connectivity and overall network performance.

The most common type of network in today's world is the Wireless Local Area Network (WLAN). WLANs are generally used for connecting multiple computers, printers and devices in one area and operating on the same wireless signal. The WLAN router is the device that receives the incoming signal from the internet and broadcasts it to the computers. A LAN is less frequently used, especially in many homes, though is still popular in larger businesses, in which there is a need for a higher level of network security and redundancy. The LAN is also sometimes referred to as an Ethernet network, although this term is used more accurately to refer to the type of cable used to connect the devices. LANs are known to provide a higher level of stability, reliability and network speed when compared to a WLAN.

Setting Email Accounts

Email accounts can easily be set up via a laptop. Most email service providers provide specific settings that users need to key into their laptop to configure their account. For example, to set up a Gmail account, enter the incoming mail server and port settings into the laptop's email system. Another popular email provider, Outlook.com, allows users to easily enter its settings via a simple website link that redirects them to their laptop's email system to set it up. The advantage to having an email account associated with your laptop is that you will be able to receive and send emails from any computer, as long as it has an active internet connection. Your laptop's email settings are associated with the account, so you don't have to re-enter the details each time.

Network Security Protocols

When it comes to wireless networking, security is a major concern. For that reason, most wireless routers come with multiple layers of security that can help protect networks from unauthorized access. The most common types of security used are WEP (Wired Equivalent Privacy) and

WPA (Wi-Fi Protected Access). WEP is the oldest security protocol, and is considered to be the least secure. It is generally only used by older devices (pre-2001) and is easily cracked. WPA has superseded WEP as the more secure protocol, using a combination of TKIP (Temporal Key Integrity Protocol) and AES (Advanced Encryption Standard) for stronger encryption. More recent routers are also capable of using WPA2 which is the strongest form of encryption available for wireless networks. WPA2 is considered to be a much more secure protocol compared to WEP and WPA as it uses an even stronger encryption algorithm. The encryption key is also encrypted rather than stored in plain text, making it even harder to crack.

Troubleshooting Network Connectivity

Troubleshooting network connectivity can be a tricky process and requires a certain level of expertise. The most common issue that arises when troubleshooting wireless networks is that the laptop is simply not able to connect to the wireless access point. This usually happens when the laptop is within signal range, but the signal strength is too low for the laptop to connect. In such cases, the most obvious solution is to move the laptop closer to the router, or to increase the signal strength from the router. If the signal strength is strong, but the laptop is still not able to connect, check for common network issues such as incorrect SSID settings, DHCP settings, or misconfigured security settings.

If these are all in order, the next step is to try to reset the wireless router and reconnect the laptop. This should solve most network issues that have been caused by misconfiguration. Sometimes the issue may be related to the laptop's firmware rather than the router. If that's the case, updating the laptop's firmware can help to address the issue. Firmware updates are provided by the laptop manufacturer and can be found on their website or downloaded from a third party source. Finally, resetting the laptop's wireless adapter can help if nothing else has worked. Overall, troubleshooting network connectivity issues can be a difficult process. It can take expert knowledge of technology, hardware and software to accurately identify and resolve the issue. If the issue persists and none of the above solutions have worked, sometimes the best option is to contact technical support.

Chapter 24: Top Laptop Brands

The laptop market today is crowded with various brands offering their own unique laptop models with their own unique advantages and benefits. Choosing a laptop brand for the purpose of purchase can be a daunting task considering that all the available laptop brands offer spectacular specs and features. In this chapter, we will take a look at the top laptop brands to help you decide on the best one for your specific needs.

Hewlett-Packard

One of the leading laptop brands, Hewlett-Packard offers a wide range of laptop models with various specs, features and pricing. Their laptops are usually stylishly designed and come with powerful processors, abundant memory, good graphics and so on. They also offer a wide selection of laptop accessories and features to help you get the most out of your laptop. HP laptops are especially good for those looking for a reliable laptop that has been designed with the user in mind, as they have a proven track record of providing excellent products.

Acer

Acer laptops are also immensely popular amongst laptop shoppers due to their good price-to-performance ratio. They offer a range of laptops with excellent specs and features, from the ultra-portable Acer Swift series to the powerful gaming laptops like the Predator series. The build quality of their laptops is often praised, with sturdy construction and sleek designs that make them visually appealing. Acer laptops are also known for their long battery life, making them perfect for those on the go who need to stay connected for longer periods of time.

Dell

Dell laptops have been quite popular for many years now, thanks to their reliability and durability. Dell laptops come in various sizes, specs and models and are known for providing excellent performance and value for money. Their Inspiron laptop line is particularly popular among users due to its good specs and features while remaining affordable. Dell laptops come equipped with the latest hardware and technology, making them suitable for those who require powerful performance and features that come with a solid laptop.

Apple Computers

Apple's Mac line of notebooks is usually the first brand that comes to mind when one thinks of laptops. Known for their good design, stylish looks and powerful specs, Apple Macbooks are popular amongst both students and professionals. Macbooks come in a range of sizes, specs and models to suit almost any laptop need. From the ultra-affordable Macbook Airs to the powerful Macbook Pros, these laptops are the perfect choice for those who need the best of the best from their laptop. They also come equipped with Mac OS X, Apple's own operating system which is known for its security, stability and ease of use.

Asus

Asus laptops are known for their great specs and features as well as their stylish designs. Apart from the usual specs, Asus laptops also come with certain unique features such as the TUF series' military grade construction and gaming-oriented features like the ROG series'—both of which make them perfect for gamers and professionals who need that little bit extra in their laptop. Asus laptops are also known for their long battery life, making them great for those who need to stay connected and productive on the go.

Lenovo

Lenovo laptops have been praised for their excellent quality, value for money and great customer service. Specifically, their ThinkPad line of laptops is incredibly popular amongst business professionals due to their reliability and durability. Lenovo laptops come in a broad range of sizes and specs, making them suitable for almost any need—from the entry level ThinkPad E series to the high-end ThinkPad P series. The keyboards on Lenovo laptops are often praised for their comfortable typing experience.

Toshiba

Toshiba laptops offer great value for money while still providing good specs and features. Their Satellite series is particularly popular due to its good selection of laptops that come in both traditional and premium designs. Toshiba laptops come with a range of features such as good graphics and sound quality, ample storage space, and some even come with a built-in Blu-Ray drive.

Samsung

Samsung laptops are often known for their visual appeal and modern design. Samsung laptops come with a range of specs and features, from the light and thin Notebook series to the powerful and gaming-ready Odyssey series. The laptop displays are also renowned for their vivid colors and sharp resolutions, making them perfect for those in need of a laptop that looks as good as it performs.

Microsoft

The Microsoft Surface line of laptops has become increasingly popular in recent years, thanks to its unique design and powerful specs. These Windows laptops come in a range of sizes and models, from the entry level Surface Go to the powerful Surface Book. They are perfect for those who need a lightweight laptop that is capable of handling demanding tasks and comes with a great battery life.

Others

The laptop market today is also filled with other interesting brands such as MSI, Gigabyte, Razer, Huawei and many more. These laptop brands offer their own unique specs and features that make them suitable for certain specific laptop needs. You can consider these brands if you are looking for a laptop that is powerful, stylish or offers great features. Once you have found the perfect laptop brand, you can start looking for the perfect laptop model. Comparing specs and features, and checking online reviews of the various laptop models can help you make an informed decision about the laptop that best suits your needs. By doing your research properly, you can easily find the perfect laptop for you.

Chapter 25: Troubleshooting Display Problems

Display Problems & Possible Solutions

When it comes to laptops, one of the most frequent problems to cause computer failure is a muddled display. If your laptop has a flickering screen that won't stay on, or a thoroughly distorted or scrambled image, or if the display is totally blank, then it is possible you are having a display problem. Fortunately, almost any display issue is fairly easy to troubleshoot. The most common cause of display issues is a worn out connection between the laptop's mainboard and its display, which is often referred to as a "cable crack". This is because the cable cracks as it expands and contracts due to the laptop's constant temperature fluctuations. Fortunately, in most cases, simply replacing the cable can be enough to resolve the display issue. If the display issue persists after replacing the cable, then there may be a number of other issues that could be causing the problem. From damaged ports to bad drivers and other types of hardware malfunctions, the list of potential display issues is endless. However, the good news is that once a competent technician has established the root cause of the issue, most types of display problems can be fixed fairly easily.

Graphics Card Issues

Another potential culprit in display problems can be an issue with a laptop's graphic card. A common sign of a faulty graphic card is a black screen, or distorted, flickering images. In this situation, it is almost always necessary to replace the graphic card in order to solve the problem. Before splashing out on a new graphics card, it is always a good idea to check for driver updates. If the graphic card is still on warranty, then the manufacturer may assist in repairs.

Resolving Dead Pixels

A dead pixel, or a "sub-pixel", is a common issue with laptop displays. It is usually caused by a fault in the LCD cell, but can also be caused by a manufacturing defect or physical damage. Most manufacturers will replace a laptop's display if a small number of dead pixels are detected, but if the issue is caused by physical damage or a manufacturing defect then this will usually not be the case. It is also worth noting that it is possible to fix some dead pixel issues using specialized software. However, this is not a guaranteed fix and will also depend on the severity of the issue.

Replacing Inverter Boards

The inverter board is responsible for controlling the backlight of a laptop's display. Issues with this component can cause the display to become unresponsive, or to terminate unexpectedly. If this is the case, then it is highly likely that the inverter board should be replaced. Replacing an inverter board can be quite tricky, and should only be attempted by those with a good knowledge of the components of laptop displays. If a replacement inverter board is not readily available, then it's best to find a technician that can do the job correctly and safely. Keep in mind that laptops can be difficult to repair, so it is best to take the appropriate precautions when troubleshooting display problems. It is always wise to consult with a professional if the issue has been unable to be resolved. Good luck!

Chapter 26: Maximizing System Performance

For users who are looking to get the most out of their laptops, understanding and optimizing system performance is key. With the right tactic and strategy in place, you can make your laptop run faster and smoother than ever before. In this chapter, we explore some techniques and best practices that can be used to maximize performance, such as examining hardware performance, optimizing software performance, analyzing system load and usage, and adjusting power management.

Examining Hardware Performance

Glitches in system performance are often caused by hardware limitations.

Even if the operating system and programs that are running on the laptop are functioning efficiently, hardware constraints can still limit the system's performance. You can quickly identify hardware issues by measuring the system's response time or throughput, which can then be used to find which hardware elements are causing the slowdowns. Before conducting any hardware tests, it is recommended to disconnect any external devices that could be bottlenecking the system. Some external components, such as portable hard drives, USB devices, or old mice, can dramatically decrease the laptop's performance if not removed. Additionally, scan the system for viruses and malware before running any tests to ensure it is free from any malicious software that could be causing problems. It is also a good idea to check the external components of the laptop. Look for dust build-up, particularly around the cooling vents and heat sink, and clean it out with an air duster or damp cloth. Also check any removable media, such as SD cards or optical discs, which can cause slowdowns if they are old and corrupted.

Optimizing Software Performance

Once you have ensured the hardware is functioning properly, it's time to check the software side of the laptop. Start by identifying programs that are causing slowdowns or crashing unexpectedly. To do this, use the "Task Manager" or "Activity Monitor" to check the system's resource utilization. This will allow you to see which programs are taking most of the system's resources, so you can address them. It is also a good idea to remove or replace any software that is not used frequently. Unnecessary programs can hog system resources and lead to a slower laptop. You can also consider disabling services and processes that are not necessary. If you need to install new software, be sure to do your research to find the most efficient option. Read reviews and compare user experience to find the best program for you. Also, check the system requirements to ensure that the software won't be too intensive for the laptop.

Analyzing System Load & Usage

To make sure the laptop is running efficiently, you should also analyze the system's load and usage. You can do this by monitoring the processor and memory utilization or you can use a system analysis tool such as "Process Monitor" or "Task Manager" to inspect the system's resources. This will help you identify any processes that may be causing bottlenecks in the system. It is also important to monitor the laptop's temperature. This can be done with a temperature monitoring app or tool to ensure the system is running at an optimal temperature. When the laptop is running too hot, it can cause system slowdowns and even hardware damage if it gets too high.

Adjusting Power Management

To reduce system load and maximize battery life, you should also consider adjusting the laptop's power settings. Many laptops offer power-saving modes, such as "battery saver" or "performance settings" which can help conserve energy and reduce the processor's load. Additionally, you can set the low-power settings to trigger if the laptop is idle for a certain amount of time. To further maximize battery life, consider wearing an anti-static wriststrap or wristwatch when dealing with laptops. Static electricity can cause damage to the delicate electrical components of the laptop, reducing its life and performance. By analyzing and optimizing the system performance and arranging a well-planned power management strategy, users can maximize the effectiveness and responsiveness of their laptops. By implementing these tactics, users can ensure their laptops are running efficiently and smoothly, allowing them to get the most out of their laptops.

Chapter 27: Optimizing System Performance

When it comes to laptop repair and maintenance, ensuring optimal system performance is an essential part of the process. In this chapter, we take an in-depth look at how to maximize the performance of your laptop or notebook device.

Examining Hardware Performance

One of the first steps in ensuring optimal performance of your laptop or notebook is to examine the existing hardware capabilities. It is a good idea to invest in a reliable diagnostic tool to inform the user of any potential faults that may be affecting performance. Additionally, by properly assessing the onboard components, such as memory, storage, CPU, and other components, the user can make informed decisions when upgrading components or performing repairs. Sometimes, these upgrades can involve buying additional parts not already included in the stock device. Although this increases costs, they can also improve overall performance significantly. Having an understanding of the purpose and capabilities of the various components helps when budgeting and planning for these upgrades.

Optimizing Software Performance

In addition to adequately assessing hardware performance, one must also consider the performance of the laptop or notebook's software. This involves examining installed applications, the OS, and other system software that can affect performance. When it comes to software optimization, it's essential to utilize the latest versions of applications and OS updates to ensure peak performance. Additionally, OS customizations should be made only when necessary and should be applied slowly, to test the impact of each change on performance. Additionally, using system optimizers to regularly clean up RAM can help maximize performance and allow for overall faster system operation.

Analyzing System Load & Usage

When it comes to laptop repair and maintenance, another important aspect of maintaining optimal performance is analyzing system load and usage. This requires keeping an eye on the onboard sensor which tracks the amount of load individual components of the system are experiencing. Graphing this data over time can help determine any patterns appearing in the data and can help identify potential problems or areas of the laptop or notebook which need improvement. Furthermore, analyzing system load and usage can help diagnose issues with hardware components and help identify faulty parts or components. By comparing before and after usage levels, one can determine in which areas the system is underperforming and make changes that will improve these areas.

Adjusting Power Management

Finally, it is important to properly manage laptop and notebook power consumption. This is especially important if one is performing heavy tasks, such as video editing or gaming. One should pay particular attention to the settings on their device of choice, as some applications and processes may demand more power while accomplishing tasks. One easy way to help manage power consumption is to reduce the screen brightness. This can result in a significant reduction in power consumption and can help extend the overall battery life of the laptop or notebook. Additionally, using power-saving settings on the device can help conserve power when on battery power or when running intensive operations. By monitoring the power usage of the laptop or notebook, making small adjustments here and there, and taking preventive maintenance seriously, users can ensure optimal performance with their laptop or notebook for many years to come.

Chapter 28: System Utilities & Software

System utility software and other programs are often essential components of laptop repair and maintenance work. Utility software helps streamline system maintenance, diagnose problems, and even optimize performance. Mastering the use of system utility software is integral to any laptop repair and maintenance job.

Installing & Configuring Utility Software

Successful laptop repair technicians understand the importance of having well-configured utility software installed on the system. It is crucial to know how to install, configure, and update system utility software on a laptop. This includes antivirus software, disk cleaners, system optimizers, and other security applications. Configuring the software correctly should be one of the first steps in any laptop repair and maintenance job. Configuring the utility software to fit the laptop's needs is essential to ensuring system performance and security. Detailed knowledge of the operating system, the laptop components, and the utility software available is a must for any laptop repair technician.

Troubleshooting Software Problems

Advanced laptop repair and maintenance work will often involve troubleshooting software problems. This can include diagnosing issues with installed programs and applications, uninstalling and reinstalling software, and resolving compatibility and configuration issues. Additionally, laptop repair technicians should be knowledgeable of common software configuration settings and repairs in order to diagnose and resolve software issues quickly.

Understanding Software Licensing

Software licensing laws can vary from country to country, and many jurisdictions have laws that are complex and changing. In order to keep up with the latest software licensing regulations, it is essential for laptop repair technicians to maintain an understanding of basic licensing requirements. This knowledge is important for dealing with clients, and ensuring the use of legally obtained software. In many cases, installation of pirated or downloaded software can result in system malfunctions, as well as potential legal liability for the laptop repair technician. It is also important to be aware of End User Licensing Agreements (EULAs) and other associated documents, as these are necessary for the installation of certain software and can help to protect the laptop repair technician in the case of any legal issues. In conclusion, understanding and maintaining system utility software, drivers, and firmware is an important part of laptop repair and maintenance work. It is necessary to have a good grasp on common software issues and licensing requirements in order to provide optimal service. Proper maintenance of laptop software can help ensure optimization of system performance and stability, and prevent common software problems.

Chapter 29: Maximizing System Performance

Preserving the performance of your laptop is essential for ensuring you are getting the most out of your device. There are a few things you can do to keep the system running at its optimum level throughout its lifetime. In this chapter, we'll discuss some essential tips for maximizing performance and keeping your system running efficiently.

Memory & Cache Management

The memory and cache present on your laptop are the system's short-term storage and retrieval capability. How much memory your laptop is installed with and what type of cache is essential to keeping the system running smoothly. With the current advancements in technology, laptop processors have gotten incredibly efficient, allowing them to access data and run programs much faster. As such, laptop owners are encouraged to upgrade the memory and update the cache on their device as often as possible to optimize its performance. Another important factor in memory and cache management is file clean up and optimization. Keeping the system up-to-date with the latest system and software updates, as well as regularly deleting unnecessary files, is essential for keeping the system running fast and efficient.

Multitasking & Multithreading

Multi-tasking is when a person or a system performs multiple actions and/or processes concurrently. Multi-threading is when multiple tasks or subsets of a task are handed over to different core components of the system. Although multitasking and multithreading have become very important in modern computing, they are also a major system resource hog. Keeping tasks and processes to a minimum, or even master managing those processes more effectively, can be beneficial in optimizing performance.

Process Management & Updates

The process management & update section of a system is what keeps it running at its optimum level of performance. This includes the system's operating system, the software installed, and all the individual processes. It is strongly recommended that laptop owners update all their software and system processes and components on a regular basis to avoid performance lags and lower the possibility of system errors.

Customizing Laptop Settings

Customizing laptop settings can also be a great way to maximize performance. In some cases, laptop owners do not take full advantage of their system's options and settings. They can, however, configure the settings to better suit their individual needs and lifestyle. For example, if gaming is the priority, then allocating more system resources to the graphic card and display, and reducing the frequency of the system's processor can give the laptop better performance when playing games. Or, reducing power consumption or battery life can be achieved by setting the screen brightness and adjusting the graphic card settings accordingly. Overall, there are many things a laptop owner can do to maximize their laptop's performance, some of which may require more technical abilities than others. Doing regular updates, memory and cache management, and customizing laptop settings are all great ways of keeping your system running smoothly, quickly and efficiently. It is always important to make sure that you constantly monitor your laptop's performance, and take the necessary steps to ensure your device is operating at its full potential.

Chapter 30: Enhancements & Accessories

Enhancements and accessories are one of the most important components for laptop computers, as they can significantly improve the performance of a laptop. With the right upgrades and external accessories, users can get the most out of their laptop and keep it running for longer.

Extending Battery Life

An important part of laptop ownership is having the proper battery life, so users can work and play remotely without needing to find a power outlet. Adding extra battery packs or using a laptop power adapter with a larger capacity will provide a longer battery life, and will help users get more out of their laptop. Additionally, adjusting power settings, like dimming the screen or disabling unneeded peripherals, will also help conserve battery life.

Adding External Accessories

In addition to the laptop itself, users can use a variety of external accessories to enhance their laptop experience. External keyboards and mice can add extra comfort and convenience, while external drives and media players allow users to store additional data and play music, videos, and other media. Additionally, various adapters and hubs can help to connect more devices to the laptop, allowing for more versatility and increased productivity.

Keeping Cables & External Storage Secure

Having the proper cables and adapters is essential for laptop usage, and can be easily stored in briefcases or laptop bags. External storage is also important, as it allows users to easily store larger amounts of data and transport it from one place to another. USB flash drives and external hard drives are great for this purpose, but keep in mind that any storage device is susceptible to data theft. To protect against potential data theft, users should make sure to implement password protection and encryption on any devices they use for external storage.

Securing Keyboard & Mouse

External keyboards and mice are popular accessories for laptops, as they enable users to work with a more comfortable setup. However, these devices are also susceptible to damage and theft, since they are not directly connected to the computer. To secure a keyboard or mouse, users can invest in locking mechanisms to help keep them in place. Additionally, adding a password-protected access control system will make sure that only authorized individuals can access the laptop's peripherals. Finally, carrying a laptop bag is essential for protecting a laptop and its accessories. A laptop bag will provide a secure way to transport a laptop, while also helping to organize all of the user's gear. Laptop bags come in a variety of sizes and styles, which will help fit the needs of each individual user. In conclusion, laptop enhancements and accessories can significantly improve a user's experience with their laptop. Adding extra battery life, selecting the right external accessories, and properly securing keyboard and mouse are all essential components for a productive laptop experience. With the right gear and the right knowledge, users can get the most out of their laptop.

Chapter 31: Display Enhancements & Troubleshooting

Enabling & Adjusting Screen Settings

Maintaining and adjusting the display settings on laptop computers is necessary to ensure optimum viewing performance. To adjust these settings, users should first open the screen brightness utility, located in the laptop's Control Panel. Once in this utility, users can select from several options to adjust both the brightness and contrast settings. Depending on the specific laptop model, other options, such as font size and color, may also be available. The screen resolution, which measures the clarity of the display, is also a key setting. A laptop's native resolution is typically the highest and most detailed setting. If this resolution isn't supported by certain applications, users can select from several lower options. It is important to note however, that lower resolutions may produce images that appear distorted or unclear.

Troubleshooting Viewing Angles

When using laptop computers, it is important that the display be properly angled for the best viewing performance. The optimum viewing angle for most laptops will generally fall between 30 and 60 degrees. To adjust the angle, users must raise or lower the laptop's display, making use of its built-in hinge mechanism. If the laptop's display becomes significantly off-angle, it is possible to correct this with most models. Simply open the display and, while supported by its hinges, gently twist it in the desired direction. This should provide enough tension to keep it in place and allow users to maintain the desired angle.

Resolving Resolution & Refresh Rate Issues

The resolution and refresh rate of the laptop's display must be adjusted in order to produce optimal clarity and responsiveness. To select these settings, users should open their laptop's Control Panel and navigate to the screen resolution utility. Next, they should adjust the slider bars to achieve their desired settings. Once these settings are selected, users should confirm that their selection has produced the desired effect. To do this, they should change the display back to its native resolution and refresh rate and then compare the resultant image quality. If changes to either the resolution or refresh rate have made the image appear worse, users should reset the sliders to their initial settings.

Enhancing Brightness & Contrast

To enhance the overall image quality of the laptop's display, users can adjust its brightness and contrast. To do this, they should open the laptop's Control Panel and select the brightness utility. Here, they can adjust the brightness and contrast settings as desired. In cases where users wish to test the display's settings, they should use a special color calibration utility. To access this, they should again open the laptop's Control Panel and then select the color calibration utility. By going through the provided steps, users can dramatically improve their display's color gamut. When adjusting the brightness and contrast settings, users should always keep in mind the laptop's intended use. If the laptop is used indoors, lower brightness settings should be used; however, if the laptop will be used in a brightly lit environment, then the brightness settings should be adjusted accordingly. Additionally, users can adjust the contrast settings to add more depth and clarity to the image.

Chapter 32: Transferring Data

From time to time, laptop users may need to transfer, store, and restore important data from one laptop to another. This could be due to a hardware failure, software issue, or just transferring data from an old laptop to a newer model. In any case, it is important to understand the basics of transferring data between laptops and other storage devices.

Saving & Transferring Data to a New Laptop

When replacing an old laptop or moving data from one computer to another, it is important to consider the many options available for transferring data. The best option to transfer data from an old laptop to a new one is to transfer the data over the internet. This can be done by transferring the data from the old laptop onto a cloud storage service such as Google Drive, OneDrive, Dropbox, Box, Bitcasa, or iCloud. With cloud storage services, users can access their data from any computer with a web browser, which makes it an excellent choice for transferring data from one laptop to another. Not only is the data transfer secure, but it also ensures that the files are stored in a safe place in case anything happens to one of the laptops. Another option is to save the data to an external hard drive. This can be done by using the laptop's USB ports to connect the external hard drive to the old laptop and transferring the data. Once the data has been saved to the external hard drive, it can then be connected to the new laptop and the data can be restored to the new laptop. This is a great way to ensure that all of your data is backed up and safe in case something happens to the old laptop.

Backing Up Data to an External Drive

Unfortunately, hardware and software can fail on a laptop at any time, which could result in loss of important data. To ensure that your data is safe in case of hardware or software failure, it is important to back up your data on an external drive. This can be done by using one of the many backup software programs available, such as Acronis True Image or Symantec's Norton Ghost. Both of these programs can be used to create a complete image of your computer's hard drive and save the image to an external drive. Once the image has been created, the image can be used to restore the laptop's data in the event of a failure.

Reinstalling Operating Systems

From time to time, laptops may need to have their operating system reinstalled to fix various software issues. When reinstalling an operating system, it is important to consider all of the data on the laptop's hard drive. To ensure that the data is safe, it is important to backup the data on an external drive or cloud storage service prior to reinstalling the operating system. Once the data has been backed up, the operating system can be reinstalled and the data can be restored to the laptop.

Securing & Restoring Data

It is important to keep data secure when transferring it between laptops or other external storage devices. To do this, it is important to use secure data transfer protocols such as SSL and TLS. These protocols will encrypt the data while it is in transit and will help to ensure that no one other than the intended recipient can access the data. Once the data has been securely transferred, it is important to ensure that the data is properly restored to the new laptop. This can be done by using one of the many data recovery software programs available. These programs can help to locate and restore lost data from various storage devices, including the laptop's hard drive. Transferring data between laptops and other storage devices can be a complicated process, but it is important to ensure that your data is safe and secure. By understanding the basics of data transfer, storage, and backup, users can rest assured that their data is secure and that any important files are backed up in the event of a failure.

Chapter 33: External Security Devices

Working with laptop computers often comes with the risk of exposure to malicious online threats and malware. Understanding external security devices and their various applications can help to protect against these risks and keep our sensitive data secure.

Understanding External Security Devices

External security devices are powerful tools which can help to protect our devices from malicious activities. These devices are typically connected to our laptops through USB and can perform a range of tasks such as tracking data transfers, encrypting data, blocking malicious websites, and even scanning emails for suspicious content. Common examples include anti-virus software, firewalls, and Virtual Private Networks (VPNs). In addition to anti-virus, firewalls and VPNs, there are also other security devices which can help to protect our laptops. These can include virus scanners, malware blockers, password managers, and malware removal tools. To keep our devices secure, it is important to understand the various types of security devices, and invest in appropriate protection.

Researching Security Standards & Protocols

Researching security standards and protocols is an essential part of protecting our laptops from online threats. Knowing which standards and protocols are currently accepted or supported by our system can be invaluable in selecting the appropriate security devices. For example, if our system does not support the latest encryption protocols or methods, then the data we are sending or receiving is vulnerable to attack. Security standards and protocols can also help to protect our laptops from data breaches and other malicious activities. By researching and understanding the security protocols used by our system, we will be better equipped to recognize potentially malicious activities and respond more quickly to any potential threats. Additionally, understanding security protocols can also help to ensure that we are provided with appropriate levels of protection.

Installing & Configuring Security Software

Once we understand the various types of security devices available, the next step is to install and configure the appropriate security software. This is an important process which should not be taken lightly. Installing the incorrect software or configuring it incorrectly can leave our data vulnerable to attack. When installing security software, it is important to consider the security protocols and standards that our system supports. Additionally, we should ensure that the security software we install is appropriately configured to provide the most protection for our data. This can include changing the default settings or configuring additional measures, such as encrypting sensitive data.

Troubleshooting Security Issues

When using our laptop computers, it is important to regularly troubleshoot any security issues. It is possible for malicious activities or threats to go unnoticed for a long time, so it is important to be vigilant. If we suspect that our system has been compromised, then it is important to take quick action and investigate the issue. When troubleshooting security issues, we should first investigate the source of the potential threat. This can often be difficult, as malicious activities are designed to be difficult to detect and investigate. However, if we think that our system has been compromised, we should look for anomalous activity on the system, such as unauthorized data transfers or unexpected processes running on the system. By understanding external security devices, researching security standards and protocols, installing and configuring the correct software, and regularly troubleshooting potential security issues, we can greatly increase the security of our laptop computers and reduce the risk of malicious activities or data breaches.

Chapter 34: Enhancing the User Experience

Increase Efficiency

One of the most important aspects of laptop repair and maintenance is increasing efficiency. By understanding how to work with specific components and pieces of software, users can make their laptop run faster and more effectively. The best way to increase efficiency is to learn how to work with keyboard shortcuts and automate repetitive processes. Utilizing an external mouse or gaming pad to control their cursor movement can also help to save time and energy, as the user won't have to use the trackpad as often.

Look for ways to reduce eye-strain

Working on a laptop can be quite tasking on the eyes, especially after long hours. Adjusting the screen's brightness and using a lighter color scheme can reduce eye strain and help your laptop become a healthier work environment. Moreover, investing in an external monitor or docking station can allow the user to spread out their work across multiple screens, which can relieve stress on the eyes.

Simplify

Amidst all of the complex processes involved with laptop repair and maintenance, users should also strive to simplify their experience. Unneeded applications, hidden files, and corrupt program components should be cleared out in order to ensure that their laptop is running as efficiently as possible. Furthermore, users should look for ways to group and organize their windows, documents, and applications so that they are easily accessible when needed.

Maximize Outlets

Optimizing the laptop's power outlets is another great way to enhance the user experience. If a laptop uses a wall outlet, make sure that it's the closest one available. Additionally, if the laptop includes a USB-C port, it can be used to charge various devices as well as power them. With a high-capacity power bank, users can even use their laptop to charge cell phones and other portable electronic devices when on the go.

Keep Security up-to-Date

Last but not least, users should always keep their security measures up-to-date. Having a reliable antivirus or anti-malware program running can help protect users against malicious attacks, while using secure passwords whenever possible will help protect their data from unwanted users.

Additionally, making sure that their laptop's operating system and software are up-to-date can ensure that security measures are as robust as possible. Learning how to enhance the user experience is one of the most important aspects of laptop repair and maintenance. By taking the time to simplify processes, maximize power outlets, and keep security measures up-to-date, users can make their laptop a much more efficient and enjoyable tool for work and play. Moreover, increasing efficiency and reducing eye strain can help make their laptop an even more effective workstation. By understanding these and other steps, laptop users can make sure their laptop repair and maintenance results in the best possible outcomes.

www.ingramcontent.com/pod-product-compliance
Lightning Source LLC
LaVergne TN
LVHW051708050326
832903LV00032B/4085